Mother Teresa

JUNIOR ▪ WORLD ▪ BIOGRAPHIES

Mother Teresa

MILDRED M. POND

CHELSEA JUNIORS

a division of CHELSEA HOUSE PUBLISHERS

Chelsea House Publishers
EDITOR-IN-CHIEF: Remmel Nunn
MANAGING EDITOR: Karyn Gullen Browne
COPY CHIEF: Mark Rifkin
PICTURE EDITOR: Adrian G. Allen
ART DIRECTOR: Maria Epes
ASSISTANT ART DIRECTOR: Noreen Romano
MANUFACTURING DIRECTOR: Gerald Levine
SYSTEMS MANAGER: Lindsey Ottman
PRODUCTION MANAGER: Joseph Romano
PRODUCTION COORDINATOR: Marie Claire Cebrián

JUNIOR WORLD BIOGRAPHIES

SENIOR EDITOR: Kathy Kuhtz

Staff for MOTHER TERESA
ASSOCIATE EDITOR: Wendy Murray
EDITORIAL ASSISTANT: Karen Akins
PICTURE RESEARCHER: Ellen Barrett
SENIOR DESIGNER: Marjorie Zaum
COVER ILLUSTRATION: Bill Donahey

First Printing

1   3   5   7   9   8   6   4   2

Library of Congress Cataloging-in-Publication Data
Pond, Mildred.
    Mother Teresa/Mildred Pond.
        p.   cm.—(Junior world biographies)
    Summary: A biography of the Catholic nun who was awarded the Nobel
Peace Prize in 1979 for her work with the poor.
    ISBN 0-7910-1755-9
    1. Teresa, Mother, 1910–   —Juvenile literature. 2. Missionaries of
Charity—Biography—Juvenile literature. 3. Nuns—India—Calcutta—
Biography—Juvenile literature. 4. Calcutta (India)—Biography. [1. Teresa,
Mother, 1910– . 2. Nuns. 3. Missionaries. 4. Missionaries of
Charity—Biography.] I. Title. II. Series.
BX4406.5.Z8P66   1982   91-12559
271′.97—dc20   CIP
[B]   AC

Contents

Mother Teresa greets students outside the Missionaries of Charity school in East Beirut, Lebanon. A civil war raged nearby, but Mother Teresa was willing to risk her life for the sake of helping the children.

1

Hearing
the Call

It was the summer of 1982. Mother Teresa, a Catholic nun, was once again pursuing her life's mission: caring for the poor, the sick, and the dying. This time, though, the situation was more dangerous than usual. At the age of 72, Mother Teresa had come to the small country of Lebanon, in the Middle East, where war had broken out. Israeli soldiers had recently invaded the country, hoping to wipe out the *Palestine Liberation Organization* (PLO) military camps in Lebanon.

This invasion had come in the middle of a civil war between *Christians* and *Muslims* that had been raging for seven years. As a result of the new attack, tens of thousands of Lebanese people were killed and wounded.

Many officials, worried about her safety, had urged Mother Teresa not to come. But Mother Teresa knew she had to go there to help. Heavy fighting had made landing at the airport in Beirut too dangerous, so she took a tiring 17-hour ferry ride from Egypt.

Mother Teresa had planned to visit the Missionaries of Charity School, which she and her *order* (religious community) had founded in 1979. But soon after she arrived, Mother Teresa put aside those plans. Instead, she wanted to cross the battle zone—called the Green Line—between Muslim West Beirut and Christian East Beirut, in order to rescue the children who were stranded there. Every government and church official she spoke to opposed her plan. It was much too dangerous, they said. "This is not just an idea,"

Mother Teresa told them. "This is our duty." Lines of experience and care etched her sun-browned face. It was a face filled with kindness—and determination.

The next day, she asked the U.S. special envoy, or messenger, to the Middle East, Philip Habib, to help her. But he only repeated the warnings she had already heard. "Mother, do you hear the shells? It's absolutely impossible for you to cross at this time." Mother Teresa told him she had been "praying to our Lady and I have asked her to let us have a cease-fire here tomorrow." Habib told her that he too believed in prayer and that if a cease-fire took place, he would arrange for her to make the crossing.

A cease-fire did go into effect the following day. Whether or not it was in answer to Mother Teresa's prayers, her strength of purpose and special sense of fairness impressed the military leaders of Lebanon. As soon as the cease-fire began, Mother Teresa asked a Red Cross official, John de Salis, where help was needed most. He told

9

her that 37 mentally ill children were stranded in a hospital that had been bombed. Explosives had blown out windows, punched holes in walls, and blasted apart the top two floors. The children would surely be killed, he said, when the fighting started again.

Mother Teresa began her rescue mission at once. She traveled to the hospital and, with the help of International Red Cross workers, carried the frightened children to four waiting vehicles. Some of the children were wounded. Cries, moans, and sobs broke the quiet of the streets. Soon the terrified children were resting in cleaner, safer surroundings. Mother Teresa worked along with the Missionaries of Charity sisters, changing bandages and giving comfort to each child.

Seeing hungry, injured, and diseased children was not a new experience for Mother Teresa. For many years she had worked long hours each day to aid victims of poverty and natural disasters, such as fires and floods. But she had never seen the horror of war. In a very sad tone she said, "I don't understand it. They are all children of God. Why do they do it? I don't understand."

Mother Teresa was born on August 27, 1910, in Skopje, a tiny town in Macedonia. (Macedonia is now a republic of Yugoslavia.) Her parents named her Agnes Gonxha; she was their third and last child. Her father, Nikola (Kole) Bojaxhiu, was a well-to-do merchant. Her mother, Drana, was a very fine seamstress.

At that time, Macedonia was part of the Ottoman Empire. Many different peoples lived in the region—Greeks, Albanians, Turks, Serbs, and others. Agnes's parents were Albanians. Each ethnic group hoped for its own independence. There were frequent uprisings. The situation was so explosive that the Balkan peninsula was called "the powder keg of Europe."

Kole Bojaxhiu was very interested in politics and served on the Skopje town council. He also joined a secret organization that worked to gain Albanian independence. In 1912 they finally won independence, and the nation of Albania was born.

The family lived comfortably. Kole, who often traveled throughout Europe on business, always brought home presents for his children: his older daughter, Aga; his son, Lazar; and young Agnes. He was a strict but loving father. He expected his children to obey his rules, but he was also willing to bend society's rules if it would help his children grow. For example, he believed that his daughters should receive an education. This was an uncommon idea at that time. Agnes's parents were deeply religious Catholics. They never turned away anyone in need, and Agnes's father often made donations to the local church.

In June 1914 the Balkan powder keg exploded. A Serbian nationalist (a person in favor of independence for the Serbian people) murdered Franz Ferdinand, the archduke of Austria. This assassination began World War I. Several years later, in 1918, while Kole was attending a meeting of Albanian nationalists in Belgrade, he became violently ill. He was brought to Skopje by carriage for emergency surgery, but he died the following day. Agnes's family was convinced that he had been poisoned by his political enemies.

Kole Bojaxhiu's death was a terrible blow to his family. He had been the family's only means of support. Now Drana was left with three young children and no income. She went to work as a dressmaker. Although she had to work hard to support her children, Drana always found the time to help the poor. Her spirit of generosity was perhaps her greatest influence on her children. Agnes often tagged along with her mother on visits to the sick, the elderly, and the lonely. Even as a young girl, Agnes showed unusually tender feelings for those less fortunate than she.

Drana taught her children about sacrifice and kindness. One day, a wealthy woman came to Agnes's home to order a dress. When the woman began to speak unkindly about someone, Drana interrupted her and pointed to a plaque over the door. It read, "In this house, no one must speak against another." The woman was so angry at being scolded by a poor seamstress that she picked up her things and walked out. Drana told her children: "We can do without money, but we cannot do with sin. Let hundreds go, but I will not allow any impurity into my heart."

The three Bojaxhiu children were very close. Both Aga and Agnes enjoyed schoolwork and reading. They also loved singing in the church choir. Agnes was a good writer, and she often wrote poems about her love of God.

By the time she was 12, Agnes firmly believed that her true vocation, or calling, was the religious life. In 1924, the new parish priest, a Jesuit named Father Jambrenkovic, arrived. He soon started a church society for young girls. Agnes quickly joined. One time the priest spoke to the girls about Catholic *missionaries*—people who travel around the world helping the poor and spreading the faith. Agnes had read about such work in Catholic magazines and surprised everyone at the meeting by standing in front of a huge world map and pointing out the locations of the missions.

In her senior year of high school, Agnes began to think about devoting her life to God. She was most interested in the Loreto order, a group of nuns who worked in Bengal, India. She prayed for guidance and, in time, came to believe that she felt God's call to join the missions in India. She decided to answer the call, although she knew that joining the order would mean leaving home. She realized she would be separated from her family, perhaps forever. But she was a determined young woman who never looked back. She later said, "I decided to leave my home and become a nun, and since then I've never doubted that I've done the right thing. It was the will of God. It was His choice."

This photograph was taken in 1928, when Agnes was 18 years old. By then she knew that she would devote her life to serving God.

2

To Learn
and to Teach

When Agnes was 18 years old, she had a single vision: to join the Loreto order. Her goal came as no surprise to Father Jambrenkovic, but it was quite a shock to her family. According to Mother Teresa, when her mother heard of her plans she closed herself in her room for 24 hours. But she soon accepted her daughter's decision. She told Agnes, "Put your hand in His and walk all the way with Him."

Agnes's brother, Lazar, and her sister, Aga, reacted to the news differently. Aga was saddened by the thought of her beloved younger sister leaving. Nevertheless, she knew it was best for Agnes to follow her heart. Lazar, by this time a soldier in the army of Albania's king Zog, learned of Agnes's plans in a letter she wrote to him. He was shocked and frustrated. He wrote to her that she would be wasting her life. Agnes replied in a strong letter of her own. "Lazar," she wrote, "you feel you are important as an official, serving a king of two million people. I am an official too, serving the king of the whole world."

As her departure drew near, Agnes wanted to store up memories of her home country. She took walks along the beautiful Vardar River, watching the sheep as they grazed on the rolling hills. A number of her friends, sorry to see her go, arranged a concert in her honor. Everyone offered good wishes for her future.

Finally, the day came for Agnes to travel to the Loreto Abbey in Dublin, Ireland, where she would begin her new life as a nun. On September 25, 1928, with her mother and sister, Agnes left home by train for Zagreb, in Croatia. (Croatia is now a republic of Yugoslavia.) After tearful good-byes, she boarded another train for the next part of her journey, to Paris, France.

A young woman by the name of Betike Kanjc, also bound for the Loreto Abbey, joined Agnes at Zagreb. After many tiring days on the train, the two young women arrived in Paris. They stayed for a short time with the mother superior of the local Loreto order before traveling on to Ireland.

The abbey, or *convent,* was a simple red-brick building in Rathfarnham, outside of Dublin. It seemed forbidding behind a barred gate, but Agnes was comforted when she saw the statue of the Virgin Mary in the courtyard.

Agnes and Betike were at the convent to study English—the language the nuns used to teach India's schoolchildren. Although Agnes found her new surroundings strange, she worked hard to learn the very different language. Clad in the long white habit, or dress, and black veil of the Loreto nuns, she spent many hours studying. Six weeks later, Agnes and Betike knew enough English to go to India. In India, they would begin their *novitiate*—the period of study and prayer a nun has before taking her vows.

Agnes and Betike left by ship on a journey to India in November 1928. The ship sailed through the Suez Canal, down the Red Sea, and across the Indian Ocean. This was the most direct route from Europe to India at that time.

In January, they sailed into the Bay of Bengal and landed in Calcutta. Calcutta, India's third largest city at that time, was probably an overwhelming sight for a young woman used to the quiet countryside of Skopje. The streets spilled over with ragged-looking people, carts, animals, and noise. Many people earned no more than a few cents a day. Some men even worked as human horses, pulling *rickshas*, or wheeled carriages, through the narrow streets. Others sold goods or services to the few people who could afford them. There were countless beggars. The city contained *bustees*, or slums. Living conditions were so horrible in these areas that many of the poor died young; the average length of life was only 30 years.

After a few months in Calcutta, Agnes was sent to the convent of the Loreto sisters in the northern part of India. The convent was located in Darjeeling, in the beautiful and peaceful foothills of the Himalaya mountains. There, in May 1929, Agnes's novitiate began. She studied Scripture and the rules of the Loreto order. She continued to study English and also began to learn the Indian languages of Hindi and Bengali. In addition, she was given instruction in teaching, the main duty of the Loreto sisters. Soon she was teaching English to European and Indian children at the convent school. Her busy days always included prayer, and she did all that she was asked with a simple, sincere heart.

On May 24, 1931, Agnes took her first vows as a Loreto nun. She vowed herself to poverty, chastity, and obedience. In a ceremony much like a wedding, complete with white dress and veil, she symbolically married Christ. She took the name Teresa, after Thérèse, the patron saint of missionaries. Known as the Little Flower of Jesus, the 19th-century nun from Lisieux, France, believed that she could best serve God by leading a life of goodness and simplicity. Like the French saint, Sister Teresa has said she longed to express her faith by going "the way of spiritual childhood,

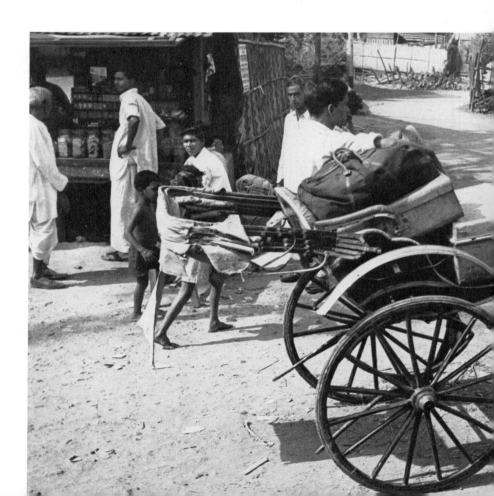

the way of trust and absolute self-surrender" to the will of God.

Sister Teresa's first assignment was at the Loreto convent school in a poor district of Calcutta. The school had taught Indian and Anglo-Indian girls since the mid-19th century. The simple but spacious buildings, surrounded by pretty gardens and stone walls, seemed far removed from the squalor and poverty of Calcutta.

A barefoot teenager pulls a ricksha *through the streets of Calcutta, India. Although the city's poor work long hours to earn money, most earn no more than a few cents a day.*

Sister Teresa's new duties included teaching geography and history to students from wealthy families. She was also assigned duties at St. Mary's, another school on the convent grounds. St. Mary's was attended by younger, poorer, and orphaned children.

On May 14, 1937, Sister Teresa took her final vows. She pledged to serve God for the rest of her life. She eventually became principal of the school, but her attention was often drawn beyond the convent walls. Although she loved teaching, she kept asking herself, Is this where God really wants me? Every day she could look out her bedroom window and see the overcrowded area of slums known as Motijhil. Disease, starvation, and misery abounded there—in contrast to the school's comfortable surroundings. She wanted to go and help those who were suffering, but the order's rule of enclosure meant that no nun could leave the convent. The only exceptions made were for nuns needing hospitalization or for those going to the annual retreat at Darjeeling.

During this period India was undergoing great changes. Mohandas Gandhi was leading a movement to free the country from British rule. Gandhi, known to his millions of followers as Mahatma, which means "great soul," wanted to achieve his goal of self-government by using nonviolent means of protest. But tensions heightened between India's two largest religious groups, the *Hindus* and the Muslims, and violence erupted. The Muslims feared discrimination in a country ruled by Hindus. They began to demand an independent country of their own. The Hindus rejected this idea of partitioning, or dividing, India. In August 1946, a massive four-day riot broke out in Calcutta, turning the streets into battlefields. Normal living routines, including food deliveries to the school, stopped.

As principal of the school, Sister Teresa was responsible for feeding her several hundred students. Although it was dangerous to do so, she roamed the city streets in search of food. What she saw appalled her. The riots had claimed the lives of 5,000 Calcuttans and injured 15,000 more. Many of the dead and injured lay abandoned in the streets. This horrifying sight strengthened her desire to work in the slums.

On September 10, 1946, aboard a train going on her annual retreat in Darjeeling, Sister Teresa experienced what she later described as "the call within a call." She was convinced that God wanted her to give up her comfortable convent life and go into the slums to help the poor. God's message was unmistakable: "I was to leave the convent and help the poor while living among them. It was an order. To fail it would have been to break the faith." To follow this new path, though, she would have to break the promise she made 15 years earlier, when she pledged her life to the Loreto order.

Sister Teresa spoke to her spiritual director, Father Celeste Van Exem, about her desire to leave the order. She told him that she wished to begin a new order of nuns to work with her in the slums. Father Van Exem brought her request to Calcutta's *archbishop*, Ferdinand Perier. The archbishop remembered Sister Teresa from when she had first arrived at the order. She had been so timid she had trouble lighting the candles. This memory colored his thinking: He did not feel she was ready for such a challenge. He told Father Van Exem that Sister Teresa must wait a year. He also said that if she left the order to work for the poor, she would not be able to do so as a nun.

Sister Teresa accepted the archbishop's decision. Fortunately, when word finally came from the highest church officials in Rome a year later, the news was worth the long wait. Not only would Sister Teresa be allowed to work for the poor in the slums, but she would be allowed to start her own order.

A young boy works on his school lesson. Mother Teresa started her first school for slum children in 1948. Her outdoor "classroom" was located beneath a small tree.

CHAPTER

3

A Missionary of Charity

On August 16, 1948, Sister Teresa removed the dark Loreto nun's habit she had worn for 17 years. The long robes, stiff collars, and head coverings usually worn by the nuns would not be right for the hot, dirty streets of the slums. Instead, she put on a simple white cotton *sari*—the traditional garment worn by most women in India—that was decorated with a blue border. She was ready to leave the Loreto convent for her venture out into the world.

Although she had looked forward to this day for almost two years, leaving the convent was very painful for Sister Teresa. She later called her departure "my greatest sacrifice, the most difficult thing I have ever done." For years, the Loreto sisters had been her only close friends. Her firm belief in God's plan for her life helped ease her sadness.

Sister Teresa did not leave for the over-crowded slums of Calcutta right away. She first traveled 240 miles to Patna to receive basic medical training from Mother Anna Dengel and her Medical Missionary Sisters. In Patna, the sisters warmly welcomed Sister Teresa. They immediately began asking her to assist them on their visits to local homes and hospitals. The nuns helped dozens of patients every day, so there was little time for detailed instruction. Sister Teresa learned by doing. During her three-month stay, Sister Teresa learned how to deliver babies, set broken bones, and give inoculations, which are shots that protect a person from certain diseases. She learned the symptoms of many illnesses and studied nutrition and *hygiene*.

Sister Teresa did not feel it was right for her to have luxuries that the people in the slums could not afford. So she planned to eat only rice and salt, which was the common diet of Calcutta's poorest citizens. When she told the sisters of Patna about her plan, Mother Dengel warned her that such a diet would make her weak. Sister Teresa saw the wisdom of this advice. She decided that she and the young women she hoped would join her would eat a balanced diet so that they would have more energy to help the poor.

The Medical Missionary Sisters were impressed by how quickly Sister Teresa adapted to her work. She was able to buckle down and tackle the important tasks first. She seemed to be able to shut out worries of every kind and to concentrate on what needed to be done.

After three months in Patna, Sister Teresa felt she had enough training to work in the streets of Calcutta. One morning in December 1948, she traveled by train to Calcutta, where she was sure God wanted her to spend her life. Arriving with no money and no place to stay, she went to see her old friend, Father Van Exem. He contacted St. Joseph's Home, where the Little Sisters of the Poor took care of poverty-stricken elderly people. The order's mother superior gladly offered Sister Teresa a place to stay.

Calcutta's problems were so huge that Sister Teresa was not sure how to begin her mission of mercy. She spent her first few days helping the Little Sisters of the Poor in their work. Finally, on December 21, 1948, she went into the streets on her new mission. Carrying only a packed lunch, she headed into the slums, without money, companions, or even a plan of action. She walked for two hours, until she reached Motijhil—the slum she had seen from her convent bedroom window. Because she had been a teacher, she decided to start a school right there, near the shacks of the poor, under a small tree. On the first day, five half-naked children came to her "classroom." There were no desks or books. Scratching letters in the dirt with a stick, Sister Teresa began to teach the children the alphabet. Within a short time, 40 children gathered around her each day. In addition to language and arithmetic, Sister Teresa taught the children basic hygiene.

Although her school thrived, Sister Teresa knew that her work was just a drop in the bucket. The problems of Calcutta had worsened in recent years. India had gained independence from British rule in 1947, and the country had been divided into Muslim Pakistan and Hindu India. But the conflict between Hindus and Muslims continued. As a result of the horrible fighting between the two religious groups, millions had moved from one region to another. The mass migration brought more riots and much bloodshed. Many Hindus, without jobs and without homes, swelled the already crowded slums of Calcutta. Doomed to a lifetime of extreme poverty, they lived in the streets, sleeping, cooking, eating, and often dying there.

Food and water became scarce. The sanitation system was unable to keep up with the

Muslim refugees crowd a train going from the New Delhi area to Pakistan in 1947. The refugees were trying to escape the horrible fighting between Muslims and Hindus, India's two rival religious groups.

needs of such large numbers of people. The food and water supply was soon polluted. Through her students, Sister Teresa gained firsthand knowledge of how families lived. The depth of their poverty shocked her. Many considered it good fortune if they obtained 1 *rupee* (about 11 U.S. cents) a day. Countless numbers of them experienced gnawing hunger every day of their lives.

Sister Teresa had no money to give; instead, she gave herself, her energy, and her love. She walked the streets looking for ways to help. Each evening she would return to St. Joseph's so exhausted she was not sure she could get through the next day. The task seemed impossible. Years later, she explained how she faced these difficult days. She said she saw Jesus Christ "in the broken bodies of forgotten people." Another time she explained: "I picked up a man from the street, and he was eaten up alive from worms. Nobody could stand him, and he was smelling so badly. I went to him to clean him and he asked, 'Why do you do this?' I said, 'Because I love you.' "

At the end of each long day, she welcomed a warm meal, sleep, and the companionship of the nuns. She wrote in her diary: "God wants me to be a lonely nun, laden with the poverty of the cross. Today I learned a good lesson. The poverty of the poor is so hard."

With Father Van Exem's help, Sister Teresa found a place to live that was closer to her work. In February 1949, a small second-floor room in the house of an Indian-Catholic family became her new home. The house belonged to a teacher named Michael Gomes, who became very helpful to Sister Teresa. He obtained medicines for her to give to the poor. His daughter, Mabel, often joined her on shopping trips to buy supplies. The entire family gave her strong moral support. No one realized it at the time, but this simple, upstairs room at 14 Creek Lane would become the cradle of a worldwide organization of immense influence.

In March 1949, one of Sister Teresa's former convent students, Subhasini Das, came to see her. She wanted to join Sister Teresa in her work with the poor. Subhasini became the first of hundreds of young women who gave up security and material possessions to help India's poorest of the poor. Other girls came soon afterward, sometimes before they had completed their education. Sister Teresa always made sure that they finished their schoolwork.

The women went into the streets each day, never knowing what they might come across. They prayed for courage and strength before going from house to house, asking for donations. They used the money to feed and treat the hungry and the sick and to support their school.

Sister Teresa was so involved in her work, she barely noticed that her first year outside the convent had passed. It was time for Archbishop Perier to decide whether she could remain outside the convent. He had heard good reports of her dedication to her mission, which now numbered 10 young women. He also knew that Sister Teresa had recently decided to become an Indian citizen.

That decision, he thought, further showed her dedication to India's poor. Mother Teresa later wrote: "I feel Indian to the most profound depths of my soul."

The archbishop decided to help Sister Teresa set up a congregation in his *archdiocese*. This would give Sister Teresa the independence she needed in her work. He asked her to draw up a constitution. She wrote one quickly so that he could take it with him on his upcoming trip to Rome. In the constitution, Sister Teresa included the three vows of chastity, poverty, and obedience as well as a fourth: "wholehearted free service to the poorest of the poor."

High church officials in Rome accepted the constitution, and on October 7, 1950, Sister Teresa became the mother superior of a new order called the Missionaries of Charity. Her official title was now Reverend Mother, but she refused the adjective *reverend* and asked to be called simply Mother Teresa. The ceremony, performed by Father Van Exem, took place in a third-floor room at 14 Creek Lane and was attended by several of the Medical Missionary Sisters from Patna.

Soon the group of young women had expanded to 26. The Gomes family kindly allowed the use of more space in their large home. Mother Teresa taught the women of her congregation to treat each person, no matter how ill, as God's child. She has written: "Speak tenderly to them. Let there be kindness in your face, in your eyes, in your smile, in the warmth of your greeting. Always have a cheerful smile. Don't only give your care, but give your heart as well."

Mother Teresa encouraged the nuns to be cheerful in their caretaking because "the poor deserve not only service and dedication but also the joy that belongs to human love."

Residents of Calcutta sit outside their tiny sidewalk homes. Generation after generation of these "pavement dwellers" are born, live, and die in the streets.

4

Helping
the Poorest
of the Poor

The Missionaries of Charity was now a reality. The girls who came to Mother Teresa faced a hard life, but they did not mind. They were willing to share a life filled with sacrifice for the sake of helping others. Like Mother Teresa, their vocation was to assist the most needy. "Vocation is like a little seed," Mother Teresa explained. "It has to be nourished. You have to keep on looking out for it. Vocation cannot be forced. The person whom Christ has chosen for Himself, she knows—maybe she doesn't know how to express it, but she knows."

Some of the young women who joined the Missionaries of Charity expected that the hardships of the slums would be carried over into their own living conditions. But Mother Teresa made sure that her nuns had enough to eat. Their rooms were simple but comfortable. Like Mother Teresa, they always wore sandals and a white and blue-bordered sari.

As the congregation grew in number, it required more space. The Gomes's house was now too small. Father Julien Henry, a Belgian Jesuit who had become Mother Teresa's trusted adviser, rode the streets of Calcutta on his bicycle, looking for a bigger building to house the missionaries.

Father Henry knew a Muslim politician who owned a large house. The politician had planned to live in it after he retired, but the city's many problems had made him change his mind. The three-story building met the sisters' needs perfectly. Archbishop Perier lent them the money to buy the house, and Mother Teresa later said: "Divine providence is always given us in unexpected ways."

By mid-1953, the Missionaries of Charity had moved into their new home. They made the house their organization's official headquarters. During this period, Mother Teresa took her final vows as the order's mother superior. But she never set herself above her sisters. Their work was her work. Together they did the daily chores—they scrubbed floors, washed mounds of bedding by hand, or cleaned maggots out of putrid wounds. Some of their charges were "filthy, covered with sores," Mother Teresa has said. "We wash them all. Of course, when a case is really too bad, I do it myself."

One day in 1954, Mother Teresa found a woman dying in the gutter. When she brought the woman to a hospital, the medical officials did not want to admit her. But Mother Teresa insisted, staying at the hospital until they did. That same day, she visited Calcutta's public health authorities. She asked them to help her provide the city's poor with a decent place to die.

Soon after, a city official contacted Mother Teresa with good news: He knew of an unused building that could serve as a shelter for the dying. It was located next door to an important Hindu shrine and had been used for overnight stays by people visiting the shrine. The next day, the sisters began to ready the building for their work. When they were finished, they named the shelter Nirmal Hriday, the Place of the Immaculate Heart.

At first, some Hindu leaders objected to the idea of Roman Catholic nuns setting up a shelter so close to the Hindu temple. The sisters, however, were not trying to get their patients to join the Catholic faith; their only concern was for them to die with dignity. Later, one of the Hindu leaders who had been critical of the shelter came to visit. After watching the sisters care for the dying with such love and kindness, he was full of admiration for the project. He told his followers:

"In the temple you have a goddess in stone; [in Mother Teresa] you have a living goddess."

Nirmal Hriday could take care of about 120 people at a time. Over the years, tens of thousands have been admitted. Inside the home, which is also referred to as Kalighat—the Home for the Dying—rows and rows of narrow cots hold dying men and women. Their faces mirror a lifetime of suffering and pain. Tuberculosis, malaria, dysentery, malnutrition, leprosy, and cancer are just a few of the causes of death inside the shelter. All of the patients are treated with loving care. Mother Teresa has said she wanted to give them "beautiful deaths. A beautiful death is for people who lived like animals, to die like angels—loved and wanted."

As they roamed the Calcutta streets caring for the poor, the nuns often came across starving and homeless children. Sometimes they found newborn babies, especially female babies, left in the street to die. Indians considered girls less valuable than boys because a girl would leave home to marry one day, depriving her family of needed labor. A daughter would also need a dowry, or sum of money, to give to her new husband. Many of these abandoned children were diseased, blind, or handicapped in some way. Often, when a poor woman died at Nirmal Hriday, she left behind children. The sisters cared for such orphans.

There were so many needy children that Mother Teresa decided to open up a home for them. In 1955, a rough two-story building, quite close to the order's headquarters, became available for rent. After renting and furnishing the building, Mother Teresa opened Nirmala Shishu Bhavan, the Children's Home of the Immaculate Heart. The home was divided into different sections. Infants who had survived their first several months rested in cribs on a lower floor, near the older, healthier children. In another room, the very sick babies were put on life-support systems. These babies were given round-the-clock care by the sisters. Toys and clothing were donated by people in the community.

Also, Mother Teresa and the sisters set up a food program for the poor. Families were given different-colored pieces of paper, depending upon their religion. Muslims came on one day, Hindus on another. It was a wise decision on the part of Mother Teresa, who understood the importance of keeping these rival religious groups apart.

Nirmala Shishu Bhavan also became home to teenage girls whose parents had either died or

Mother Teresa plays with orphaned boys and girls at Nirmala Shishu Bhavan. She and the sisters try to bring joy to these children to make up for the hardships they have suffered.

deserted them. These girls faced a dangerous life on the streets, but in the home they were safe. The sisters taught them useful skills, such as sewing and typing, so they would be able to care for themselves. In return, the older girls helped the sisters care for the younger children. Whenever a girl received an acceptable marriage proposal, Mother Teresa saw to it that she had a small dowry to take with her, even if it was only a simple bed or towels.

Some people criticized the work of the nuns at Nirmala Shishu Bhavan. They said the money would have been better spent on population-control programs than on nursing poor children. Mother Teresa disagreed: "God gives what is needed. He gives to the flowers, the birds, and little children his life. There are never enough of them. God made the world rich enough to feed and clothe all human beings."

Mother Teresa was also deeply touched by the suffering of still another group—the victims of leprosy. Leprosy, known as Hansen's disease, has plagued mankind for centuries. The disease destroys skin and nerve tissues, and unless it is detected early, it causes severe deformities. Dangerous infections occur on the skin, and gangrene, the death of tissue, can spread rapidly. Sometimes hands and feet must be amputated to stop the gangrene from spreading. The disease is not highly contagious, but so-called lepers have nearly always been treated as outcasts, even by their families. Hindus in India believed that people with leprosy had done some evil deed in a past life, which caused their present miserable existence.

In 1957, there were about 30,000 victims of leprosy living in Calcutta. Many of them were outcasts, chased away from their homes and jobs. One day a small group of them visited the only person they knew would care: Mother Teresa. After talking with them, Mother Teresa realized the time had come to create a program for them. She knew that sulfone drugs and a proper diet could improve their health within a year, and if the disease was discovered early enough, many

Elderly victims of leprosy welcome Mother Teresa upon her visit to the St. Lazarus Leprosy Village in South Korea in 1985. Mother Teresa feels that each person, no matter how ill, deserves recognition as a valuable human being.

could even be cured. The Missionaries of Charity set up several clinics at key places in the city. But many leprous people could not walk to the clinics or were too embarrassed by their deformities to be seen by a doctor. So Mother Teresa figured out a way to bring treatment to them. She filled a van with medicine, food, disinfectants, bandages, and other needed supplies. Then, with two sisters and a doctor, Mother Teresa rode in the narrow streets looking for infected families. Once they were found and treated, each person with the disease was given an identification card. These patients were then given food and medicine every week.

In time, Mother Teresa founded Shanti Nagar, the Town of Peace—a community for people with leprosy, located on 35 acres about 200 miles outside Calcutta. Of the nearly 400 families who live there today, most are able to support themselves. Thanks to Mother Teresa, they have been trained in such skills as brick making and handicrafts. Shanti Nagar is now run independently of the Missionaries of Charity, but it continues to follow the goals of Mother Teresa. Every day, the people there are enriched by a program that recognizes their importance as individuals. This attitude has always been at the heart of Mother Teresa's work: Each individual has equal worth in the eyes of God and deserves recognition as a valuable human being.

Mother Teresa and a sister kneel in prayer. She and her Missionaries of Charity sisters always wear a simple white and blue-bordered sari and live without luxuries.

5

The Mission Grows

Mother Teresa once said, "Calcutta can be found all over the world if you have eyes to see." She was speaking of the countless numbers of neglected, unwanted people in every country of the globe. Rejected by society or forgotten by their friends and family, they suffer the greatest poverty—loneliness. After Mother Teresa became aware of this kind of suffering, she could not ignore it. She wanted to ease the loneliness in the world, and she wished to expand the work of her Missionaries of Charity in India and in other countries as well.

The first mission outside Calcutta was set up in 1959, in a poor district called Bihar. To get there, Mother Teresa and her team of sisters had to travel more than 200 miles. This was the first of hundreds of such teams that would, in the years to come, fan across the globe to help others.

The expansion of the Missionaries of Charity was funded by donations from wealthy Indians and supporters overseas. Many of the contributions were the result of Mother Teresa's travels. In 1960, she made a whirlwind tour of the United States. She gave speeches in a number of American cities, telling her audiences how they could help the needy in distant countries. Her listeners gave generously. In New York City, she met with high church officials and numerous civic leaders and made a visit to the United Nations. While touring one of New York's depressed areas, she saw men staggering from alcohol and drug abuse. It upset her to see so much suffering in such a rich nation. She was also saddened that no one stopped to help these people.

After leaving the United States, she traveled to England and Germany, where she received many more contributions. The size of the gifts, she has always said, is less important than the act of giving. "To show great love for God and our neighbor we need not do great things. It is how much love we put in the doing that makes our offering something beautiful for God."

Mother Teresa traveled on to Rome, where she planned to make a special request of the *pope*: that he grant the Missionaries of Charity official recognition. She wanted her order to be under the authority of the Holy See instead of the archdiocese of Calcutta. (The Holy See is the pope's seat of power.) This change would permit her to expand her mission throughout the world. Papal recognition, however, was not to come for four years, a delay Mother Teresa accepted with great patience.

While in Rome, Mother Teresa enjoyed a warm reunion with her brother, Lazar, who had settled in Italy after World War II and raised a family. Missing from the reunion were her mother and sister. Mother Teresa had not seen them since she left Skopje in 1928. Her many efforts to get them out of Albania, strictly controlled by a Communist government, had always failed.

By 1962, 119 Indian women had joined the Missionaries of Charity. Many of these nuns were sent to set up new missionary houses in more than 30 locations in India. Within a few years, the Missionaries of Charity houses spread from the snowy Himalaya mountains in the north to the hot tropics of southern India. Among other facilities, the sisters set up a home for the dying in Delhi, houses for the poor in several other cities, and a leprosy clinic in Patna, where Mother Teresa had learned her medical skills.

In every new house, the sisters followed the same daily routine that Mother Teresa had set up for them in the original house in Calcutta. The sisters arose at 4:40 A.M., put on a sari and sandals, and went to chapel for prayer, meditation, and mass. They ate a simple breakfast of tea and the flat Indian bread known as chapati, then began their work with the dying, the orphans, or the leprosy victims. After attending chapel for prayer at 6:00 P.M., the sisters spent their evenings together. This spirit of community was very important to Mother Teresa. It gave the sisters the sense of family she felt was the essence of the order. By 10:00 P.M. most of the sisters were in bed. Mother Teresa often used the late hours to answer the many letters she received.

As her congregation grew, Mother Teresa realized that it would be good if men could be organized to do the same type of work as the sisters. On March 25, 1963, 12 young men and a priest joined what would become the Missionary Brothers of Charity. In the decade that followed, the brothers went to work in war-torn areas such as Vietnam and Cambodia. Mother Teresa felt that these places were too dangerous for the sisters to work there. Today there are hundreds of male missionaries in 44 houses around the world.

Mother Teresa would have preferred to stay home in India than spend precious time traveling and talking to the press. But she knew these trips helped the poor, for they spread the message of urgent need to the four corners of the earth.

In February 1965, the Missionaries of Charity was granted papal recognition. The order, which at the time numbered 300 women, would be able to expand its work into the rest of the world. Within five months the sisters had set up their first center outside India. It was in a small village in the South American country of Venezuela. A team of sisters found an old snake-infested, abandoned hotel, cleaned it up, and went to work. The people they served, mostly women and children, were descendants of African slaves.

The first centers outside India, like those that followed, were learning experiences for the sisters. The people they helped were from different cultures, with customs and needs that had to be met in new ways. Mother Teresa never gave her sisters specific rules to follow. She knew that with God's help they would find ways to give their love to those who needed it. During the late 1960s and 1970s, at least 10 new outposts of the Missionaries of Charity were established in South America.

In 1966, Mother Teresa left Venezuela to travel once again to Rome. She wanted to renew her efforts to help her mother and sister leave Albania. She met the Albanian attaché in Italy, who assured her his government was looking into the matter. Two years later, however, her mother died, and Aga did not survive her for long. Mother Teresa was very disappointed that she never saw them again. But she took joy at the thought that her beloved mother and sister were with God.

In 1968, Pope Paul VI surprised Mother Teresa with a request: He asked her to bring a team of sisters to help the poor who lived on the outskirts of Rome. Many of these people lived in run-down buildings without heat, electricity, or running water. Once she became convinced that they truly needed help, Mother Teresa established a Missionaries of Charity center in Rome.

That same year, Mother Teresa received an invitation to visit Tanzania, a country on the

Mother Teresa and Pope John Paul II greet a welcoming crowd on her visit to Rome in 1986. Mother Teresa set up a Missionaries of Charity house in Rome in 1968.

east coast of Africa. President Julius Nyerere wanted to teach his people to become self-supporting. He did not want to single out any group as poor or in any way inferior, so Mother Teresa referred to the needy there as "our people." The sisters converted some old buildings into a home for the elderly, nurseries, a medical supply area, a kitchen, and a meeting room. Within these walls, abandoned children received care and blind and sick old men and women were fed and bathed.

By 1969, Mother Teresa realized that many *lay people*, including non-Catholics, wanted to help, too. That is, they wanted to contribute more than money to Mother Teresa's cause. With the help of a British woman named Ann Blaikie, who had supported Mother Teresa's cause for years, a new group was formed: the International Association of the Co-Workers of Mother Teresa. Co-Workers meet regularly to share their experiences and pray together. Also, Co-Workers agree to live as simply as they can in "voluntary poverty," which means sacrificing luxuries.

When many sick people wanted to become Co-Workers, Mother Teresa formed a related group, the Sick and Suffering Co-Workers. Their main duty is prayer and correspondence with the Missionaries of Charity. Mother Teresa has a special outlook on suffering: She feels that the sick experience more of Jesus' sufferings than do healthy people and so have a greater compassion, or feeling, for those who suffer. By 1985, the Co-Workers numbered 2,600.

The noble work of the Missionaries of Charity did not go unnoticed. In 1971, Mother Teresa was given the first Pope John XXIII Peace Prize from Pope Paul VI. He praised her for her work with the poor, her Christian love, and her efforts on behalf of peace.

The Missionaries of Charity continued to grow. They set up a center for the aborigines—the natives of Australia who had been pushed off their land by white settlers. Mother Teresa described a special visit with an old aboriginal man: "There was in that room a beautiful lamp, covered for many years with dirt. I asked him: 'Why do you not light the lamp?' 'For whom?' he said. . . . I asked him: 'Will you light the lamp if a Sister comes to see you?' He said: 'Yes, if I hear a human voice, I will do it.' The other day he sent me word: 'Tell my friend that the light she has lighted in my life is still burning.' "

Mother Teresa and her sisters also brought their services to other developed countries. The first of many U.S. Missionaries of Charity houses was opened in New York City in 1971. It is located in a poor, crime-ridden section of the South Bronx. In this convent, as elsewhere, Mother Teresa insists that the sisters live simply, without the extra comforts life can offer. She believes that all who would help the poor must experience poverty themselves.

Nobel Peace Prize winners Archbishop Desmond Tutu and Mother Teresa exchange kind words. Mother Teresa visited South Africa to open a House of Charity in a black township near Cape Town.

6

To Do Small Things with Great Love

In 1971, Mother Teresa turned 61, an age when most people think of retiring or at least slowing down. Mother Teresa, however, continued her hectic schedule. In 1972, she and her sisters went to the aid of the people of Bangladesh. The tiny country had just been formed, when East Pakistan declared its independence from the rest of Pakistan. Civil war had broken out after this declaration, and more than 3 million people were killed when troops from West Pakistan moved into Bangladesh.

More devastation followed the conflict—famine, poverty, and homelessness. The country of Bangladesh became known as an "international basket case." Mother Teresa and the sisters were among the first charity groups to arrive and offer help. She and the nuns went to work burying the dead, tending to the wounded, and hiding many young women from troublemaking soldiers. Also, they arranged for families in Europe to adopt many of the orphaned babies. Eventually, four Missionaries of Charity centers were established in Bangladesh.

Mother Teresa was honored with India's Nehru Award in 1972 for her efforts in Bangladesh and around the world. The Indian president V. V. Giri described Mother Teresa as an "emancipated soul who has transcended all barriers of race, religion, creed and nation."

One area where this was especially true was the Middle East. The region had seen three major wars. There was constant friction between Israel and its Arab neighbors, who did not recognize the Jewish state as being legitimate. After the Six-Day War in 1967, the Israelis had captured and occupied the West Bank, an area west of the Jordan River. Thousands of Palestinians who lived in the area fled into Jordan. In 1970, Mother Teresa and five sisters established the first missionary house in the Jordanian capital of Amman. A short time later, a civil war erupted. When calm was restored, the sisters tended to the wounded and the homeless.

Similar refugee problems had resulted from the 1967 war in the Gaza Strip, a slice of land between Egypt and Israel. In 1973, after the bloody Yom Kippur War, the Missionaries of Charity set up a mission to aid some 380,000 Arabs who had fled into Gaza during the fighting.

Mother Teresa was invited at this time to bring a team of nuns to another Muslim nation—tiny Yemen, at the southwestern end of the Arabian Peninsula. The Yemen government hoped the missionary sisters would serve on staff at a new hospital. But one of the order's rules stated that the sisters could not staff an institution, so Mother Teresa had to decline the offer. The team of sisters did establish a clinic, a home for the poor, and an asylum for the mentally ill in Yemen. When the Yemen government presented Mother Teresa with a "sword of honor," she laughed good-naturedly and then exclaimed, "A sword, to me!"

On still another mission, the sisters went to help the poorest of the poor in Cairo, Egypt. There the nuns helped the men, women, and children who scrounged for a living at the city's garbage dumps.

It was an amazing accomplishment for a Roman Catholic nun and her sisters to be invited into Muslim countries such as Jordan and Egypt. Wherever the sisters went, however, they did not preach their faith. Their main goal was to guide people to become the best they could be, no matter what their religion was.

The world was beginning to watch Mother Teresa. She was given numerous awards. She was the subject of many articles and even a film, *Something Beautiful for God.* The press followed her wherever she went. Mother Teresa accepted the publicity not for herself but for the poor. She wanted to draw attention to the world's poor and to report on their goodness and the need to care for them.

In 1975, the Vatican asked Mother Teresa to attend the World Conference of the International Women's Year. The conference was held in Mexico City. While there, Mother Teresa spoke about women in poverty. She urged all women to have a special concern for poor women, on whom poverty places especially crushing burdens. During conference breaks, Mother Teresa visited the poor of the city. The Mexican government learned of her visits and asked her to set up Missionaries of Charity houses there. Mother Teresa accepted the request. Over the next few years, missions opened in five other Latin American nations: Guatemala, Haiti, Panama, the Dominican Republic, and Honduras.

The Missionaries of Charity continued to set up missions abroad, but they were not always successful. In 1972, for example, Mother Teresa and four Indian sisters traveled to Belfast, in Northern Ireland. She wished to bring a message of sharing and unity to the Catholics and the Protestants, who had been hating and fighting each other for many years. Her plea was ignored, and Mother Teresa soon left.

Over the years, Mother Teresa has faced other problems. Some of the sisters have broken their vows and left the order. Some nuns have even left so they could marry. Although these departures have disappointed Mother Teresa, she accepts them as the will of God. There have also been critics of her projects. Some have said that the Missionaries perpetuate, or feed, the cycle of poverty. They claim her work is only a bandage, not a cure. It would be better, they say, if Mother Teresa aimed at the causes of poverty. Mother Teresa expressed her point of view to a newspaper reporter: "Somebody said to me, 'Why do you give them fish to eat? Why don't you give them the rope to catch the fish?' " Mother Teresa went on to explain that the poor people she and her order reach are far too weak and needy to "learn to fish." They can barely stand, much less hold a net. When the poor become strong enough to leave her, she believes, there will be someone to teach them to fish.

On December 9, 1979, an inspiring sight greeted Mother Teresa when she got off the airplane in Oslo, Norway. Thousands of cheering followers stood in the freezing weather, each holding a lighted candle. They wished to honor the 69-year-old nun, who had come to receive the Nobel Peace Prize. Perhaps the world's greatest honor, the Nobel Prize has been given to such leaders as Albert Schweitzer, the medical missionary, and Martin Luther King, Jr., the civil rights leader. In her acceptance speech at the ceremony that evening, Mother Teresa insisted that "people must love one another so no one feels unwanted, especially the children." Her wise words were met with loud applause.

Throughout all the glitter and praise, Mother Teresa remained humble. For the first time in the history of the Nobel Prize, the traditional banquet had been canceled—at Mother Teresa's request. She asked that the projected cost of the dinner—$6,000—be donated to the poor.

Three months after the Nobel Prize ceremony, her adopted country of India awarded her its highest civilian honor, the Bharat Ratna—the Jewel of India. In 1985, the United States expressed its great appreciation by giving her the Presidential Medal of Freedom. The medal was presented to her by President Ronald Reagan.

These awards and honors by no means signaled to Mother Teresa that her work was finished. In 1987, she and her Missionaries of Charity set up *hospices* in California and New York for victims of acquired immune deficiency syndrome (AIDS). Speaking engagements, educational efforts, and her ongoing work with the poor kept her far busier than she ever dreamed possible.

Despite her failing health and advanced age—in 1991 she turned 81—Mother Teresa continues to travel to places and people in need. In 1990, she went on a two-month journey through the newly liberated countries of Eastern Europe. She made arrangements for the opening of three new Missionaries of Charity houses in Albania, where her mother and sister had lived. She was still recovering from a serious illness she suffered the previous year, but as always, she was determined. With the establishment of these new facilities, the number of Missionaries of Charity houses climbed to about 450 in 95 countries.

In 1990, Mother Teresa told a reporter, "My doctors are always telling me that I must not travel so much, that I must slow down, but I have all eternity to rest and there is so much still to do. Life is not worth living unless it is lived for others."

Chronology

1910	On August 27, Mother Teresa is born Agnes Gonxha Bojaxhiu in Skopje, Macedonia.
1928	Agnes leaves Skopje to join the Loreto order in Rathfarnham, outside of Dublin, Ireland.
1929	Agnes arrives in Calcutta, India, to begin missionary work.
1931	Agnes takes her first vows and adopts the name Sister Teresa; she begins teaching at the Loreto convent school in Calcutta.
1937	Sister Teresa takes her final vows.
1948	Sister Teresa leaves the Loreto order to begin work with the poor in the slums of Calcutta and opens her first school for slum children.
1950	Sister Teresa becomes mother superior of her own order, the Missionaries of Charity.
1953	The official headquarters for the Missionaries of Charity is established in Calcutta.
1954	Mother Teresa establishes Nirmal Hriday, the Place of the Immaculate Heart.
1955	Mother Teresa opens Nirmala Shishu Bhavan, the Children's Home of the Immaculate Heart.

1959	Mother Teresa expands the work of the order within India.
1960	Mother Teresa tours the United States, giving speeches about the need to help the poor.
1963	The Missionary Brothers of Charity is founded.
1965	The Missionaries of Charity are given official approval by the pope and begin to set up missionary houses outside India.
1968	Pope Paul VI invites Mother Teresa to work in the slums on the outskirts of Rome; the president of Tanzania asks her to help the poor of his country.
1972	Mother Teresa receives India's Nehru Award and aids the people of Bangladesh.
1979	Mother Teresa receives the Nobel Peace Prize and the Bharat Ratna, India's highest civilian honor.
1987	Mother Teresa establishes hospices in California and New York for people with acquired immune deficiency syndrome (AIDS).
1990	For two months Mother Teresa journeys through the newly liberated countries of Eastern Europe.
1991	Mother Teresa opens three new Missionaries of Charity houses in Albania.

Glossary

archbishop In the Roman Catholic church, a high-ranking bishop (religious official) who heads an **archdiocese**

archdiocese a group of churches that is governed by an **archbishop**

Christians those people who profess to believe in the teachings of Jesus Christ

convent a community of nuns; also the building in which such a community lives

Hindus people who follow Hinduism, the main religion of India; Hindus believe in many gods

hospice a shelter that provides care for people who are ill or dying

hygiene the science of maintaining health

lay people   people in a church community who are not religious officials

missionary   a person, often a member of a religious **order**, sent on a mission to do charity work, especially in a foreign country

Muslims   people who follow the monotheistic (one God) religion of Islam, which is based on the teachings of the 7th-century prophet Muhammad

novitiate   the period of study and prayer a nun undergoes before taking her vows, pledging her life to God

order   a religious community

Palestine Liberation Organization   PLO; an organization dedicated to the protection of Palestinian rights and the furthering of Palestinian interests

pope   the person who is head of the Roman Catholic Church, and is also the bishop of Rome, Italy

sari   the traditional garment worn by most women in India; the sari is fashioned by draping several yards of lightweight cloth over the body so that one end forms a skirt and the other a shoulder covering

Index

Mildred M. Pond, a former reporter for the *New York Times*, is a freelance writer, playwright, and short story writer. She received her education at Hunter College and holds a master's degree in philosophy from Fordham University. She resides in New York City.

Picture Credits

DATE DUE